SEAL YOUR OWN FATE

Estate Plan Essentials to Ensure a Smooth Road Ahead

I0468430

K.D. Marley

DEDICATION

To my family and friends, and to all the families out there trudging the end

of the road, however well or poorly paved it may be.

An Old Irish Blessing

May the road rise up to meet you.

May the wind always be at your back.

May the sun shine warm upon your face,

and rains fall soft upon your fields.

And until we meet again,

May God hold you in the palm of His hand.

TABLE OF CONTENTS

ACKNOWLEDGMENTS

To: Chandler Bolt, James Roper, Self-Publishing School, and the

Mastermind Community

Thank you so much for getting this book out of my head and onto paper.

Thank you to my writing buddy Mary Kay, my Editor Nick G. and my cover designer Kay, who made this book better than it was. And thank you to my friends and family for supporting me through this process.

INTRODUCTION

So, you've made your estate plan and you are feeling pretty good about it. Think about it some more. Do you have a plan for what your loved ones will do when they get the call that you have suffered a fall and are in a coma? That your memory is so bad now that you can't take care of yourself? That you have died?

If you can honestly answer yes to all of these scenarios, fantastic! You're well ahead of the game.

But have you thought about what can go wrong with your plan? Are you feeling comfortable that everything is handled because you went to an attorney (or downloaded forms from the Internet), answered the questions, and signed on the dotted line? Did that really cover everything? Are the recommendations you received (if any) suited for your particular situation?

How will the people who find you incapacitated know who to call? Did you choose the right person for power of attorney? Did you make your wishes clear enough? Are the documents you signed adequate to cover everything? Do you know? My parents thought they had it all covered. So did I.

Estate plans are good at assuring people that they are covered in their time of need, but are not really geared toward making life easy for those left behind.

I feel very fortunate that my parents put together a pretty good estate plan, and that both sides of our blended family were supportive and wonderful through the whole process. On the flip side, I feel somewhat unfortunate to have been unprepared for the many things that weren't included in the plan, and all of the things that made being a trustee frustrating, infuriating, confusing, and just plain difficult.

The purpose of this book is to let people know that a standard estate plan is a good thing; but a great plan, one with more thought given to the actual process of both illness and dying, can be so much better for all involved.

This book is not for everyone. It is not for those who want to let nature take its course or who think they will handle it when the time comes, or who believe that everything will just work out.

This is for those who have put together a standard estate plan and wonder whether it is enough to ensure that their wishes will be honored and their loved ones cared for. This is for those who have seen or experienced how poorly many estate plans cover real-life experiences and want something better for themselves and for those they will leave behind.

My parents' estate plan covered who would make decisions for them, where their money would go after death and included a burial plan, of sorts. It also included some information about how they wanted to be treated if they became ill or incapacitated. The trouble is, a standard estate plan is like a highway filled with potholes: You can travel it, but the missing pieces can make the journey very bumpy and uncomfortable for all concerned.

Wouldn't you rather have a great estate plan? Those left behind will love you even more for it. A great estate plan is a freshly paved highway ready for smooth travel. A great estate plan provides the resources necessary for your loved ones to care for you in your time of need, the confidence of knowing what you want done when you begin to need assistance, knowledge of how and when to bring your friends and loved ones together to celebrate your life, and the time to savor the remainder of your life on earth together.

My goal in sharing some of my experiences and lessons learned on my parents' end-of-life journey is to help you to think about your estate plan in a different, expanded way, and to make a real plan for your life during your last years, months and days, and for the people you will leave behind after you've gone from this Earth. This book is for people who want to give peace of mind to their loved ones when the crisis occurs and make the transitions in life as seamless as possible.

Before I received the call that my Dad was incapacitated, I thought I was prepared to handle the details. I couldn't have been more wrong. It turned out that my parents' estate plan was not that great. My parents had prepared a trust with their attorney, which was good, but as my brother, stepsister, and I traveled down the road on my parents' end-of-life journey, the ride was distinctly and painfully bumpy. I would like to help save others from the same fate.

Once Dad was no longer there to care for my Mom, it became apparent she was incapacitated by Alzheimer's disease and I hadn't even realized it. I had known that she was ill, but I didn't understand how far her disease had progressed. In hindsight, I can see that my ignorance was a combination of Dad's attempts to compensate for her shortcomings and my willingness to remain in denial. As a result, there was no real plan for dealing with Mom's situation. This book will provide tips to help you prepare your loved ones for the crisis, provide the tools they will need to help out with your needs, and to build a solid foundation of empowerment so they will be able to handle your matters with as little resistance as possible from the outside world and from each other.

A standard estate plan will act as a guide to take care of some end-of-life business, but may leave your loved ones vulnerable to an ongoing onslaught of bureaucratic nightmares, legal paperwork, and stress. A great plan will free your loved ones to spend time with you in mutual support, and will ensure that the decisions made on your behalf are those of your choosing. You have the power to free your loved ones from the agony of not knowing what you want and the lasting guilt resulting from making decisions about your life and care in ignorance of your wishes. By re-thinking your plan to take your unique life and situation into account, not just some standard forms and legal advice, you allow this difficult time to be lightened by bonding and sharing memories with your loved ones, allowing your legacy to be one of love and support.

Because of the planning done in advance, I was able to make at least some of the decisions that I knew my parents wanted, and to handle enough of their financial matters to care for them through the end of their lives in a certain measure of comfort.

The downside of the plan was that there were so many decisions to make and matters to handle that were not covered. My siblings and I were forced to spend precious time and vast amounts of emotional and physical energy wrangling with bankers, brokers, the Social Security Administration, and the California Department of Motor Vehicles, while also trying to find contact information, medical information, and personal information. All of that time and energy would have been much better spent with my mother in her last months. These experiences taught me valuable lessons that I would like to pass on to others.

This book will help you to take a broader view of your plan, and of the possibilities for problems with it, so that you can take care of those you love now, making it easier for them to take care of you later.

Don't be the person who spends their last days alone while their loved ones are at the bank trying to make a plan for your finances, at the lawyer's office trying to figure out what they are supposed to do, or searching your old emails hoping to find contact information. Be ready now!

When the time comes, have your plan ready so that you can have your loved ones hold your hand, take care of your bills, call in your other friends and family, and make the necessary decisions knowing that they are doing what you want. There is no time to wait! While we always hope it will not happen, you may need your plan tomorrow, and it will be so much better for everyone if you are ready!

The things I didn't know made everything so much more difficult after my father fell ill. In this book, you'll find tips for turning your standard estate plan into a great estate plan. Read on to find out how to leave your loved ones with the tools they need to navigate all of the bad pavement and precarious potholes on your end-of-life highway, and allow them the freedom to spend whatever time is left for you on this earth offering their love, support, and joy to you and to others.

MEDICAL POTHOLES

Our parents' end-of-life journey started suddenly and painfully with medical questions for which we had no answers. A little planning may save your loved ones from similar painful decisions.

In our case, our mother had Alzheimer's disease which had advanced to the point where she could not assist with information or advice. So, when my stepfather suddenly lapsed into a coma, the decisions were left irrevocably up to me, my brother, and my stepsister, with me holding the power of attorney.

The nature of the end-of-life journey is often unsure and filled with gray areas, making it innately difficult to travel. However, many of the issues I faced could have been handled in advance if they had been more carefully considered. I am hoping that sharing my experiences will help you to patch up some of the potholes in your own plan so that your loved ones' issues with your medical care may be more readily and less painfully resolved.

In my case, many of the solutions to the medical issues I faced were solved by luck; some good, some bad. Will you have good luck? I don't recommend counting on it.

Since my parents lived in a small town with only one hospital, and my brother had already taken my parents there for unrelated reasons, we did not need to wonder which hospital my parents preferred.

If you live in a city with many hospitals, you will need to let your trusted person know which hospital is your choice, and which doctor you prefer, if any. This may be included in your current plan. The great plan will include having your trusted person (whom you will consider carefully in the "trust" chapter) meet the doctor and having you sign a consent form for your trusted person to receive your medical information. The discussion with your doctor should also include how the medical power of attorney works in your state and locality so that there will be no surprises.

Fill out the worksheet included with this book and make sure your trusted person knows where to find it. In my mother's last months, she did not get to see the doctors and other therapists that she would have liked to see. My mother had always been keen on alternative therapies, and near the end of her journey she was telling me that she wanted to go somewhere. Based on the context of our conversation, I believe that my mother was trying to tell me that she wanted to go to an alternative practitioner she had seen before, but she was unable to express to me who that person was, or where they were located. That was a sad day for me. I have a suspicion that since Dad did not believe in that kind of thing, he had not been taking Mom to those kinds of practitioners since she had lost her ability to go on her own.

Mom's regular doctor was also an issue. I talked to my brother and found out that Mom was now seeing his doctor. I don't know how that came to be. My brother had a stroke years earlier and was unable to speak. He can communicate reasonably well by text messaging, but communication is difficult and incomplete at best, because the communication centers in his brain were affected by the stroke. So, my mother knew this doctor was not her doctor, and she didn't like him, but she couldn't tell me who the right doctor was. It would have comforted both of us to have been able to see a person who knew her and whom she liked. Pass this information on before the crisis happens if you want people to know how you want to be cared for.

I can now think of some ways I may have been able to figure out who her doctor was, such as looking at canceled checks or old medical insurance and Medicare records, but I didn't think of that then. Keep in mind that the mind does not work at peak performance during crisis times, so planning in advance is crucial if you want the decisions made on your behalf to be those of your choosing.

My parents had Medicare and good supplemental insurance, and I held the powers of attorney, so those things were great and we thought we had everything covered - but we didn't.

Dad's Fall

My Dad fell and hit his head and, by the time I knew about it, he was in a coma. The tough decisions followed quickly and, while the Power of Attorney I had was helpful in the sense that it showed that I was entrusted to make decisions, it gave no real guidance on what those decisions should be.

The Power of Attorney said that if three independent doctors agreed that Dad would not recover, then he would not want to have extraordinary measures taken to keep him alive. Well, that sounds lovely, and it might be something that could come up after a lingering illness, but it certainly didn't happen that way for us. The day following Dad's fall, there was only one doctor and he declined to give any opinion at all.

When we got to the hospital, Dad was on a ventilator. While the decision was difficult, my stepsister and I were both quite sure that Dad would not want that, so we had it removed. He was able to keep breathing on his own, so that hurdle was cleared.

The next decision was more difficult. He was being fed intravenously, and the doctor told us that for longer periods of time intravenous feeding was not an option. If he were to continue receiving nourishment, a feeding tube would need to be inserted into his abdomen, which would require surgery.

We had a family meeting with the doctor and his expert medical opinion was that you never know what might happen. So much for doctors being wise and all-knowing! Fortunately, I have never thought that they were, but I know that some people do, so be forewarned and forearmed.

The doctor kept showing us pictures of the inside of Dad's head, as though we could understand what the meaning of that was, and asking us what we wanted to do, without giving us any opinion about it or guidance.

I finally thought to ask him what he would do if it were his father, and he said that he thought he would have the feeding tube inserted and wait about three weeks to see if he made progress; so that's what we did. We had no way of knowing if that was what Dad would have wanted or not.

That was the last decision we were asked to make for Dad before his passing. After a couple of weeks, Dad did not awaken, and his body stopped processing the food that was being fed to him, so the doctors at the hospital made the decision to remove the tube without needing to ask us about it.

They told us there was no point in continuing if it wasn't being absorbed at all and it would just cause him pain. They told us that they had him medicated so that he was unlikely to feel any pain or hunger.

I asked the nurse if the drugs they were giving him would keep him from waking up and she told me no, that the people around him that were awake and talking were on the same dose of the same medications.

So, I understood then that he could not wake up, and I could only hope that they were right about him feeling no pain. We visited, I sang to him and held his hand, my brother brought him a radio and played country music for him around the clock. He would have liked that.

So, that is how my Dad passed away.

As hard as this process was for us, it was blessedly short, and many people have much more difficult and numerous decisions to make every day for their loved ones who are no longer able to decide for themselves. Sometimes the decision-making process goes on for years.

I hope you will relieve the burden on your loved ones by making as many of these decisions as you can in advance.

Mom's Memory

The decisions for Mom were a bit easier for me because we had discussed these matters over the course of my lifetime. Although her mental capacity was severely reduced, she still would express herself, and her thinking was not always so different than it had been when she still had all of her faculties.

I highly recommend discussing these matters regularly with your loved ones. Don't get me wrong, we didn't spend our time together discussing sickness and death; it was simply a subject that was discussed for maybe 10 minutes every couple of years. My mom was smart.

Mom didn't like doctors much and would not want ventilators or feeding tubes or anything that would prolong her life. She had a great faith in God and felt that she would go when it was her time. However, since she was full-on into Alzheimer's disease, doing what she wanted was hard to figure out at times.

I went up for lunch with Mom each Friday after Dad passed away, and we would handle appointments and whatever needed to be done. One Friday a few weeks after Dad passed, I was driving, my brother and his fiancé were in the back seat, and Mom was in the passenger seat. She seemed to be having more trouble breathing than usual so I asked her if she felt alright.

She said she thought she needed to go to the hospital. We were glad that she was willing to go, since we had been unsuccessful in convincing her to go to the doctor prior to this. It turns out she had a small heart attack. They checked her out and kept her a couple of days, but when they wanted to do further testing to find out exactly what the problem was, she refused.

I thought she probably would have refused even if her mind was working properly, so the doctor and I went with her decision. She was released and we went home.

The next time she went into the hospital was after she had moved to an assisted living apartment. She wasn't feeling well, and they called an ambulance. She had suffered another heart attack.

She was angry that they wouldn't let her leave the hospital when she wanted to leave and she adamantly refused further tests. I asked the doctor what we could do because she didn't want to be treated and she had a right to her own decision, I thought. He said that, considering her dementia, he didn't disagree with me, but the assisted living facility was required to send her if she had attacks of any kind, so I should consider hospice.

I had heard of hospice, but didn't really know what it was. I did know that my Mom didn't want to go back to the hospital any more, and that she was ready for her end, however it might naturally come.

I was told by people at the hospital that Mom would have to move to a nursing facility to receive hospice, which greatly distressed me, since she had already moved and it was hard on her. Plus, in her younger days, she'd had a serious fear of nursing homes. But then the wonderful director at the assisted living facility told me that they were allowed by law to have 12 hospice patients in the facility at any time, and they currently had none. The only requirement was that we use a particular hospice organization previously chosen by the facility. As long as Mom was in the hospice program, they would not need to call an ambulance when she fell ill; the hospice workers would care for her right there at home.

I was so happy that Mom was able to stay in her apartment. She had become familiar with the nursing assistants there and had come to accept their presence. I didn't want to move her again. However, as time went on, she needed 24-hour care, and the facility did not offer that level of care. But we were again blessed by the facility's director, who was always willing and able to make decisions and work things out. She was amazing!

Many of the young certified nursing assistants at the facility wanted additional work hours, so the director talked to them and made up a schedule. We were able to have one of them there at all times with Mom until the end.

Don't get me wrong, this was expensive. But thankfully my mother and stepfather had done well with their money and had enough to take care of this situation. The money would not have lasted much longer, but it lasted as long as it was needed.

So, we went on hospice. I say "we" because hospice not only takes care of the person who is ill, but also supports the entire family. For those unfamiliar with hospice, it is a service separate from other medical services, and provides end-of-life care. Hospice begins when the decision is made to stop treating any diseases and the sole goal becomes making the patient as comfortable as possible.

A hospice team is assigned to each case. The team makeup may differ from place to place, but in my Mom's case it included a social worker, a doctor, a nurse and a few certified medical assistants.

Hospice is permitted to use medications that are not allowed in other care situations, specifically morphine. However, Medicare will no longer pay for some medications once hospice begins, so it is important to find out what the specific treatments are that will be removed. For instance, my mother had emphysema, and used an Albuterol inhaler.

Once hospice began, the inhaler was no longer covered by Medicare. I disagreed with this decision, since it seemed to me that not having the inhaler would make her totally uncomfortable because she wouldn't be able to breathe without it. I was planning to just go ahead and buy the inhalers but, after some discussion with the hospice workers, we found alternatives which worked even better than the inhaler. She was able to receive nebulizer treatments a few times a day and she began receiving morphine which, it turns out, has a magical ability to help a person breathe. Who knew? The things you learn at the end of life.

One of the happiest moments for me was when I took Mom back to the assisted living facility from the hospital that last time. When we got her back to her apartment, she said with great relief, "It feels so good to be home." I had been so afraid she would be angry with me for moving her to the facility from her home, and that one statement from her freed me from the doubt and guilt I had been feeling. I knew then that her apartment had become a comfortable home for her.

So, we traversed her medical issues, one at a time, with great stress and uncertainty. If you can make this process easier for those who will accompany you on your end-of-life journey, I hope you will do so. The time will be so much better spent for everyone.

What could be more important than your loved ones knowing how you want to be cared for in your last days? Knowing who you want by your side on your journey, that's what!

Who do you want by your side while you are ill? Who do you want to comfort your loved ones, to go to your memorial, to handle particular issues? Well, if your trusted person doesn't know who to contact, you may not get what you want, and the people you love may miss out on your journey altogether. Read on to get ideas on problems that may arise and how to avoid them.

CONTACT POTHOLES

An issue that we ran across at the start of this process and which plagued me through to the end was that we did not know how to reach friends, family, clergy, and whomever else my parents would have wanted contacted for the various stages in their journey.

When the crisis occurred, we needed to contact my parents' family and friends. This is a hard thing to think about when you're in shock and fear about the future. Thankfully, I had an email list I had prepared for an 80th birthday party I had hosted a year prior and was able to reuse that list. Without it, I would have had no idea who to contact.

I told everyone on that list what had happened to Dad, and asked them to spread the word. That brought in a rush of support ... mostly.

There were questions and even a little anger because who can word an email like that without upsetting someone? I'm rather matter of fact, and one person didn't like my suggestion that my dad was not expected to survive. I feel bad about that, but it was the truth as I understood it.

Dad had been helicoptered out of their small town to a major neurological medical center about two hours away After the decisions about his care were made and it was time for him to leave the hospital, we decided to have his further care handled in their hometown, since it would be very difficult to bring Mom to see him so far away. We had him brought back by private ambulance and the trip was hard on him, so he ended up back in the emergency room instead of the rehab. Of the many people I had advised of Dad's illness on the email list, at least three were people from my parents' church. I can't tell you how wonderful it was to find three of their friends from church in the hospital waiting room when I got there to see Dad.

It was a real comfort to find them wanting to know how Dad was, wanting him to get better, and in their love for him being devastated in finding out that he was in such bad shape. I loved that they loved him.

Remember that your loved ones will need all the support they can get, so make sure they know how to contact your friends and other family members in your time of need. Let them know about one another while you are still well and healthy.

Unrelated to the subject of this book, but a wonderful and healing thing that came up, was that one of those friends told me that the night my dad died, this friend had a dream that Dad came by and waved to him and said, "Let's go to lunch" in his usual way. He felt then that he was okay, and it also gave me great peace. In my teens, my father came to me in my sleep after he passed on, so I know how comforting that experience is. Even if perceived as being only a dream, the comfort is fully real.

Because I was not involved in their day-to-day lives, I didn't know much about contact information for my parents. I lucked out in having the email list.

However, there were people missing from the list, namely family members on Dad's side of the family who I did not know, or know about, who hadn't been invited to the birthday party because they lived far away or for other reasons.

Fortunately, Mom and Dad had a network of friends and family and the people who I notified passed the word along. I must say that it as a bit weird to notify family and friends of bad news by email, but I didn't have phone numbers. I guess in the long run that made it a lot easier on me anyway.

I recommend that you think about who you want contacted in the event of your illness or death, and how you want them contacted. Write it all down for your trusted person to use. When I say "trusted person" I am referring to your power of attorney person, trustee, or executor of your estate. This will be discussed further in the "trust" chapter.

Does anyone know your online passwords and user names? Facebook now has a way to add a legacy contact to take over your account when you pass away. Use that. My stepfather had a Facebook account and it is lost in the ether, along with both Mom and Dad's email accounts.

Dad had an SBC email account and I didn't even know who to contact about that, since SBC is no longer in business. I contacted Google requesting access to my Mom's account and, despite having a big plan and process set forth on their website, which I followed, they never even bothered to grace me with a reply.

So, if you think your loved ones might want or need to access your accounts, give them the information while you can.

I can't stress enough the importance of this step of passing on your contacts. Nobody can help your loved ones as much as other people who love you, and nobody can make their life a living hell like a person who loves you and wasn't told that something has happened to you!

Also, I was never able to get my act together enough to flesh out my email contact list, so it would have been helpful if it had been put together properly beforehand. I didn't really have "contacts," but rather an email message that I would open and "reply all."

This is a bad method. When people wanted me to add them, I would add them to the next email, but after that, I sometimes went back to my original email and left out the people I had attempted to add. I hope they all understood that I didn't intend for it to happen that way. Who knows what they think of my performance at this point? In the midst of a crisis, we do the best we can. You can help now to make the best your loved ones can do, better.

Remember to keep your loved ones in the loop on small things also. Who does your hair? Your nails? Who cleans your house? Which restaurants do you frequent? Who do you like there? All of this information may not be needed in your case, but it was needed in mine. If your loved ones need it, they will be happy they have it. This does not require constant communication, but just keep information in one place and let your trusted person know where it is.

At my parents' house was a little cork board and, while it had very little information, there was a business card there for a beauty salon. It was so nice to be able to bring my Mom to a woman she recognized and who was already familiar with Mom's condition and what she liked in a haircut.

While Mom was unable to say what she wanted, and perhaps did not know, she sure knew what she didn't want. Knowing where she had her hair cut was another pothole in Mom's end-of-life road that I was happy to avoid! The small details make life so much easier for all involved.

We were also familiar with my parents' housekeeper, so we did not have to wonder about that. But we didn't know about the restaurants. We found out about the people at the restaurants as we went along.

Each time I would take Mom to lunch I would be surprised to find that the people there knew Mom, wondered what happened to Dad, gave us great service, and knew what Mom liked to eat. These things are important in times of crisis. Let your trusted person know about all of these things.

The lesson learned here is to make a list of the people who are important to you and specify how you want each person involved in your life. Otherwise, that old friend of yours that you want by your side may never even know that you are in need. And, let's be honest here, maybe we don't want that creepy uncle that you have avoided for years giving a speech at your memorial! Let's pave over those contact potholes hiding in your road!

So, now that you have set up that contact list, let's move on to the biggest and most frustrating source of stress in my mother's end-of-life journey - the banks. Did you know that when you are incapacitated and your loved one goes to your financial institution for you, they may get treated as though they were robbing the bank? I didn't either. I do now.

BANK POTHOLES

The banks hold all the cards, or at least all the money. It is important that you involve your trusted person in your financial relationships as early as possible. Dealing with bankers on another's behalf will not happen without some advance planning.

Now, you may be thinking that you have no money so this section won't apply to you. Well, your loved ones can just as easily be spending time trying to figure out what funding is available through government, charity, church, or local services. They can be trying to figure out where you will live and who will take care of you. So, I urge you to read on anyway.

Whether you have money or not, there will be endless work that must be done to take care of the necessary tasks. Work done in advance is far less stressful than work done during the crisis, and frees up time for your loved ones to spend with you during your final months, weeks, and days, instead of fighting the bureaucracies, regardless of the status of your financial resources.

On the other end of the spectrum, you may be thinking that none of this will be a problem because you are wealthy and have hired people to handle everything for you. Well, I suggest that you look carefully at the plans that have been made and see how solid they really are.

If you hire someone to handle your affairs, you need to be able to trust them and they need to know what you want if you hope to have things go as you wish at the end of your road. Will all of those people you hired work with your loved ones or treat them like prey? Will the hired help block your loved ones from making decisions they know you would want but you forgot to tell the hired person? Will these people make your loved ones' efforts to enjoy your last days more difficult?

If not carefully chosen, a hired person may serve themselves or outside interests better than they serve your loved ones, and may not really fill the bill when the crisis comes. With the difficulties I faced with the moderate means my parents had, I can't imagine how much worse things may have been if I had been dealing with multiple banks and numerous organizations wanting forms filled out and appointments made.

I was amazed and disconcerted at the number of demands made upon me during my parents' last days. Don't let your loved ones be so surprised. With wealth also comes greater risk of fraud and theft. Be wary of those entrusted during times of vulnerability. Choose wisely and choose while your faculties remain whole.

Before discussing the need to ensure that the right person has access to your banking information, I feel the need to say a word about keeping the wrong people out of your bank account. We thankfully did not encounter this issue, but I know that theft and fraud are rampant in our society and it is very difficult to know who to trust.

My only advice would be to choose as carefully as you can and do not wait until you are in failing health because your judgment will decline over time. Make your decision now!

If you don't trust your own judgment **or those who love you suggest to you that your judgment may be lacking**, seek out counsel from someone above reproach. It may help to choose someone you have known for a long time so that you have personal experience of their honesty and integrity.

About a year before the crisis hit, my dad saw it coming. He didn't know that he would be the first to go, but he knew that he was having trouble taking care of Mom, and I don't think he felt that great either.

He gave me the binder containing the trust that he and my mother had put together years earlier, and he brought my brother and I down to the bank and had us added to their checking account as signers.

We all thought that was enough. We were wrong. I could write checks on the account and deposit funds, but I could not gain online access, get a debit card, or make any changes to the account.

Also, being a signer is not very useful if you don't have any checks! Although getting checks is not that difficult during normal times, it was impossible when we needed the first ones during the crisis. That left my sister and I to pay the first bills on our own.

It was a little weird to get checks anyway. My mother wouldn't let me get at the checks, because in her Alzheimer-addled mind she could not see why I would need those, and the bank would not allow me to purchase checks because I was not the account holder.

Of course, the bank's cautiousness was pointless, because it is no problem to order checks through an independent check provider. Later, I was able to take the checks Mom had when she wasn't looking. Anyway, the point is that it is important to sit down with a banker and get clear on what you need to do to allow total access to your trustee. When my parents were incapacitated and could no longer make decisions, the bank treated me like a thieving intruder. And, in the case of Mom's checks, do you really want your loved ones to have to trick you into letting them help you once your good judgment has gone?

I realize that dementia or Alzheimer's may not be a problem in your life, but extrapolate out to the problems you are likely to have based on your history and your family history and think hard about the situations your loved ones may encounter in caring for you.

Luckily for me, during my brother's time living near my parents, he had gained on-line access to our parents' account so that he could help Dad put their bills on auto-pay. Mom had always taken care of the household bills, and Dad did not like having to deal with that once Mom no longer was able. I am ever thankful for my brother helping them out and getting us access to their account.

Without that access, I don't know how I would have managed their finances. I would not have known how much money I was working with and so would likely have overdrawn the account and made quite a mess of things. It would have also used up even more of my time with Mom. Online access made life much easier. I highly recommend setting that up for your trusted person.

We had another issue that was unique to our situation, but it may be something to think about in your planning. When we received the life insurance money, my brother took Mom to the bank to deposit it and Mom suddenly had a bout of mistrust. She yelled at my brother, telling him to get out of the bank until finally he did, and then Mom deposited the check, opening a new account to which only she had access.

Oddly, the only reason I knew what had happened at the bank that day is that the woman I had previously spoken to called me and told me what happened. I guess her humanity overcame her bank's ridiculousness for that moment. It did not extend to giving me access to the account, but she did provide me with the account number.

I was able to bring Mom to the attorney's office later, and she trusted the attorney and me enough to sign the papers necessary to add the account number to the trust so we would be able to access it after her passing. See? Isn't this fun!?

I don't know if there is a way to get the bank to ensure that your loved ones will have access to all of your accounts, but it is a good idea to discuss this in advance. Be forewarned that my Mom and Dad's bank refused to accept the power of attorney, and the trust attorney I hired told me that this is common problem. Talk to your banker and have your trusted person added to your accounts in a way that will enable them to do what is needed when the time comes.

Some investigation showed that in addition to Social Security, my parents each had an annuity. I went to the brokerage and talked to the agent to find out what would happen with the money now that Dad had passed on. Would Mom keep receiving that income?

We learned that Mom would keep receiving her own annuity, but it was very small and almost empty.

For Dad's annuity, Mom needed to file paperwork to cash out his annuity. Once again, the fact that I had a power of attorney didn't help at all. Dad's power of attorney expired upon his death, and Mom's power of attorney was pretty much useless in this situation, as it had been at the bank. Unless we went to court to have Mom declared incompetent, she would need to sign. I had no interest in putting either of us through that nightmare, so we worked around it.

Fortunately, I was able to get Mom to cooperate in the process. Unfortunately, this is when we discovered Mom had lost her ID card. That will be covered in the "government potholes" chapter of the book. When we were able to cash out Dad's annuity, we found that it also included some life insurance, so that was a great help, particularly since the primary life insurance money was deposited in that no-access account my Mom had opened a few days earlier.

I thought the problem with the banks would be the worst part of preparing for Mom's end-of-life journey. But that was before I found out about dealing with the government. Big surprise, right?

The next chapter will cover some of the pitfalls and potholes given as free gifts by the Department of Motor Vehicles, the Social Security Administration and, to a lesser extent for me, the Department of Veterans Affairs.

GOVERNMENT POTHOLES

I am sure it will surprise you that the government caused problems in my parents' end of life journey. The government is usually so accommodating! Oh, wait, no it isn't.

There can be so many government potholes on the end-of-life road. I ran into only a few but still found them very time-consuming and difficult. Yours may be much worse, but the minimum will almost certainly occur.

During my mother's last months, we made trips to the Department of Motor Vehicles, the Social Security office, the United States Postal Service and, while we didn't personally visit the Department of Veterans Affairs, I spent time reviewing, filling in, and mailing all of their forms.

We were lucky that we had Mom and Dad's Medicare cards and they had Medi-gap insurance, and they had those cards in their wallets. If they had misplaced that information, we would have had to wrangle with those departments, too. Make sure your loved ones know where the information is kept!

United States Postal Service

For postal matters, since my mother had Alzheimer's disease, we were presented with some issues that were particular to that disease.

I'd like to share one story here as a cautionary tale which can apply to any vulnerable person in the many guises in which fraud masquerades. Dad told me this story because he did not know what to do about it. Sad to say, I was unable to help him.

Mom was a lifetime subscriber to Reader's Digest. For my whole life, there was always a Reader's Digest on the living room table. So, even when she could no longer pay attention long enough to read, she still had the subscription. That was fine. The problem was that she started receiving scam mail from someone who called themselves Reader's Digest and the mail looked official.

We called Reader's Digest to ask them to stop sending the letters and they told us that the letters were not theirs, and that they were actively seeking to stop the scam.

The letters told Mom that she was a winner and that all she had to do to claim her prize was to send in money. So she did. After that she received letters regularly telling her that she had completed one phase in the process. To move forward, they said, she just needed to send some more money, and some more, and some more.

Dad tried to tell her it was a hoax and they were stealing her money, and I tried to convince her too, but no amount of coaxing would keep her from sending the checks. She would become distraught when we tried to discuss the issue, and she would say if she didn't send the money, she wouldn't win and would lose all the money she had invested. It was distressing and frustrating.

Beware of those who prey on easy targets and school your trustee about these dangers.

I found out later that while Dad was alive he solved the problem by having a friend of his steal the mail before my Mom saw that it had come.

After Dad died, however, the mail started coming again. I didn't know about the prior arrangement, so the problems started anew. Fortunately, although Mom held on to the "Reader's Digest" mail, she either couldn't hold a thought long enough to send the money, or after the long hiatus from receiving the mail, she had forgotten about sending them money.

Anyway, Mom held tightly to her mail, and would let me look at it, but wouldn't let me take it. She went through it over and over and stressed and fretted about it. I wanted to relieve her of the burden of mail that she could no longer handle or comprehend.

Much to my surprise and relief, when I asked her straight out if I could forward her mail to myself so I could handle it for her, she said yes.

The forms from the USPS had two hurdles for us, one obvious, the other not.

First, we needed Mom's signature. When dealing with an Alzheimer's victim or otherwise uncooperative person, a signature can be a difficult item to obtain. I was lucky because, although Mom didn't believe that I was her daughter, she thought I was her friend, and her behavior usually reflected complete trust, so that made my job much easier.

Since your scenario may turn out different, I suggest you be proactive and consider how your loved ones might deal with mail delivery for you. Having access to the mail is vital for just about everything.

The second mail pothole was invisible. The USPS form gives you the option of temporary forwarding or permanent forwarding. I chose temporary, because I was not at all sure what direction we were headed in this new world I found myself inhabiting. I am so glad I did.

Temporary mail forwarding runs for a year. Once I knew that my Mom would never need her mail, I changed it to permanent. I only found out upon expiration that "permanent" only lasts a year also. How is that not temporary? Once this period is over, you cannot request another forward. So, make sure you take care of all necessary business before a year.

It would have been nice to have known about how this worked in advance, and I feel very fortunate that it didn't cause more problems than it did. As it turned out, we received only one more bill after the forwarding expired and it was a small one that I paid myself long after the trust was closed.

Department of Motor Vehicles

The California Department of Motor Vehicles (DMV) was the next fun adventure. More than a year before his fall, Dad told me that their doctor had said that Mom would no longer be allowed to drive. Dad had a very hard time stopping her from driving. Being four hours away, I was not able to help, but my brother took over and took them wherever they needed to go.

I never found out what made Mom stop driving, but she finally did. I think Dad may have appealed to her Puritanical streak by making it clear to her that it was against the law for her to drive now. Then she received her driver's license expiration in the mail and she understood.

She would rail about it and say that she was going to get it back, and it really made her angry , but she didn't drive. My Mom's rule-abiding nature made life easier in that way. Dad told me that the last time she drove, the pharmacy called him from town to say that his wife was there and she didn't know where she was or why she had gone there. He fetched her. I am so grateful for Dad taking care of Mom; I only wished I could have understood how to help him before it was too late.

So, by the time the crisis occurred, Mom was no longer driving, and my brother told me she had an ID card. In searching for her ID card, we found her expired license, so were able to use that to identify her to the DMV.

Make sure your trusted person has a copy of your license or ID card so that information will be available if needed. All 50 states and Washington, D.C. have websites with motor vehicle information for consumers. Some states have separate agencies for drivers licenses and vehicle registration, so check with your state and get an online account. Share your login information with your trusted person to make their journey easier. For Mom, I think if I had a login I would have been able to renew her ID card online and receive a replacement through the mail.

At any rate, Mom had lost or thrown out her ID card so I had to take her to the DMV to get another one. Without the ID card, I was unable to complete any banking or close out Dad's annuity. I mention that she may have thrown it out, because she had begun throwing out many things, like her hearing aids. One day she was wearing them, the next she swore she had never had hearing aids. Such fun.

We would also have needed the ID card for the life insurance, but the broker was a friend of Dad's and knew who Mom was and took care of the claim without the need for identification. I have never been one to mix friendship with work, but my opinion has changed quite a bit. My parents' friends who handled their affairs made everything so much easier for me. This may be something to consider in your planning.

Now, taking an uncooperative person to the DMV is an interesting challenge. Since my Mom's issue was that she didn't understand, it was like working with a small child, but if the person is angry and stubborn, what then?

Keep in mind that each of us may become that angry and stubborn person when we are old and/or sick, so plan for that possibility. While we waited, Mom kept trying to leave. She said, "I'll be outside when you're done" and I kept having to bring her back reminding her that this was for her. The woman who helped us was thankfully very kind and patient. Unlike the banker and some of the creditors and other vendors, she didn't try to make things harder for us and was very loving to Mom and encouraged her through the photo-taking process. We got the ID and I held onto it.

With the DMV in the rear-view mirror, we moved from small annoyances to larger nightmares. Our next stop was the Social Security Administration.

Social InSecurity

Social Security has seriously disappointing procedures. The Social Security potholes I found were: 1) How quickly it stops when one spouse dies; 2) What the new income will be; and 3) Where it will go.

If you are single, the holes I encountered with my parents should not be an issue, but you will likely find others. The most important thing that springs to mind is to have your trusted person involved in assisting you in protection against fraud. There are predators out there who will be happy to take your Social Security checks and, if your mind starts to go, you may not be able to distinguish friend from foe.

For married couples, when one spouse dies, their Social Security does not cut off immediately, it cuts off a month prior! What kind of crap is that?!

Our trust attorney told us that when a spouse dies the other spouse gets the larger amount of the two salaries. I also heard this on an estate-planning radio show, and from other people I know. After Dad passed away, Mom's first check was the same amount it had always been, which was about 1/3 of what my Dad used to get, which meant that her income had been decreased drastically, and that she was not receiving the larger of the two checks. I called the Social Security office to ask about why mom wasn't receiving the larger portion. I was advised that to adjust her income, we would need to come in for an appointment. So, Mom and I headed off to the Social Security Office.

Well, Mom did not get what Dad got, and the representative denied that there was any rule that said that she would. But, when they reviewed Mom's case, they realized that she had a prior husband, my birth father, who had passed on almost 40 years earlier. Since my stepfather was now gone, she was eligible to receive her prior husband's share. Since my father had died young, he didn't have much Social Security banked so that added a whopping $14 more a month to her check. Whoopee!

I am so thankful that Mom and Dad had good life insurance and that there were survivor benefits on Dad's annuity because that Social Security cut in pay was drastic. The result was that Mom's expenses were the same as when Dad was alive, and her income was much, much, smaller. Keep this in mind when planning.

Another hassle that came up in the Social Security meeting was that the agent asked Mom a lot of questions, and she couldn't answer any of them. In familiar surroundings, she would have been able to answer most of them, but the strange place must have confused her.

At the end of the questioning, the guy told us the he can't give Mom any money because she is unable to answer the questions. Great I thought, I brought her in here only to get her cut off completely! Someone would have to be appointed to handle her money for her. I asked him what I needed to do to get that process rolling and had the worst-case scenarios running through my head with Mom not receiving any money and spending endless hours in court and so on.

Thankfully, my doom-and-gloom prophesies were cut short when he asked Mom who she would like to have handle her money and she pointed at me. What a relief! If she hadn't, another bureaucratic nightmare would have begun. Providence had once again plucked me from the abyss.

The process of handling the money for a person on Social Security was not too bad. The agent gave me paperwork that I took to my bank. The banks have a special kind of account for this situation. This turned out to be a happy circumstance that made it easier for me to pay her bills, and the money came straight to an account that was available to me online and on paper, so I was then able to handle Mom's financial life alongside my own, which cut out some of the extra steps I had been taking to get things done.

Having traversed the harrowing process of the Social Security Administration, it was now time to tackle the Department of Veterans Affairs. I hear daily in the media about how this country does not take care of veterans. I had not had any experience in this area, but the brief contact I had after my Dad passed away was certainly unsatisfactory.

Department of Veterans Affairs

After my Dad passed on, I heard that the Veteran's Administration had burial benefits. Some investigation led me to The Department of Veterans Affairs, which is a separate organization from the Veterans' Administration. I had no idea there were two organizations. So, I filled out the "Application for Burial Benefits." The forms weren't available online, so I had them sent to me in the mail. It was a huge packet of typical government information to fill out one small form. Trying to read the directions would make Einstein feel like an idiot, so I just skimmed them and filled out the form.

There was a letter in front of the packet that was also impossible to understand, but made one point clear - you probably won't get what you are applying for. Now that strikes me as truly absurd. Certainly no private business would get even one customer with that sales pitch. Apply I did, but get it? I did not.

As with Social Security, there was no clear reason for denial, and there was an appeal process, but I had a full-time job and a mother with Alzheimer's living more than four hours away from me. The costs were not great for the headstone, and since it was Dad's money, and these were his wishes, I decided that we would go ahead and pay for Dad's burial with the money he left behind.

He did get a plot in the veteran's section of the cemetery and a nice headstone.

If you have children or other loved ones who will be responsible for you in an emergency, find out about any government entities that may be useful for your care and familiarize yourself with their procedures, and then pass the knowledge on to your trusted person.

If you have no money, or reasonably expect to run out of money before death, government assistance may be needed. Find out what is available. Don't leave it to your distraught, grieving loved ones to wade through the government bureaucracy. At least give them as much of a head start as you can.

If you already receive any kind of government assistance, give the information about the government program to your trusted person and talk to the agencies involved to find out if there is anything you can do to get your trustee in the record as a person who can take over for you.

The government bureaucracies are often time consuming and difficult to traverse. I had troubles with the DMV, the Social Security Administration, and the VA. There are so many other possibilities to anticipate, depending on your situation.

Your loved ones may need to deal with federal agencies such as Medicare or the IRS, or state agencies such as those which provide medical or other funding, or state tax collectors. It is important that you consider those that may apply to your particular situation.

With the government, the worst part was thinking we understood the situation and finding out that our information was wrong when we most needed it. In the next chapter, I will discuss housing issues, where the worst problem is that people just don't give it enough thought. Most people I have talked to think they are going to stay in their own home until they die peacefully in their bed. Is that what you think? Well, if you want that to be even vaguely likely to happen, you best plan ahead. And, will that even be what you want when you need more care than you can receive there?

Read on to find some of the issues that need to be considered to ensure that your housing in your later days is acceptable for you and your loved ones when the crisis hits.

HOUSING POTHOLES

Many times in my life, starting pretty young I recall, my mother would ask me to promise that I would never put her in a nursing home. My answer was always the same, "Mom, I can't promise you that, but I promise I will do all I can to keep that from happening. " She would always say, "I know, okay. " I am so happy that I was able to keep that promise not made. She was able to go into an assisted living facility and also received hospice care there, so she was able to stay in her new home until the end of her days.

My parents planned to stay in their home until the end of their lives. Dad pretty much made it there, at least until he was in a coma.

What we all need to consider, though, is whether staying at home is what we really want, especially when we get to a point where we need things that we can't get there. Dad loved his home, but in the end it was too much for him to care for, and it was too isolated when his mobility became limited.

We need to give thought to what we will want when we become less mobile and active, where we will want to be when we need help from others. To be frank, I don't like to receive help from anyone. However, if you need help, you need help. So, after seeing what my parents went through, it makes sense to give some thought to what you may want if your situation changes and take steps to ensure that you have the opportunity to choose what kind of help you want, when, and from whom.

For you, the options for housing may involve a high-end, specialized community where you buy in and are cared for to the end, or it may involve living with a family member or friend, or a nursing home. I urge you to seek out the probabilities and possibilities that are unique to you so that you find the best possible option.

A year or so before the crisis, Dad asked me for help. I understood then that the crisis was coming, because he was not the kind to ask for help. I did not, however, know what to do.

I began searching online for possibilities and found that assisted living might work for them, since Dad would still be able to have his freedom and Mom would get the help she needed, and they could still stay together.

Two things here: If I had been armed with all of the information I needed, I would have known that they had long-term care insurance and could have brought someone in for several hours every day to spend time with my Mom to give Dad a break. The other thing is that there was an awesome assisted living facility right in their town. But I was unaware of both.

Knowing about these two things could have eased the journey, and simply knowing all of their financial information, and doing some advance footwork in town, would have made that process possible, and Dad may have lived a bit longer, and enjoyed it more. We were too late for Dad, which makes me terribly sad, but we did find a place for Mom after Dad passed.

It was not clear to me how ill my Mom really was until Dad was taken from us. My brother had moved up near them a year or two earlier to help them out, and now that Dad was no longer there to care for her, my brother moved in with Mom.

My brother may have understood the nature of her illness sooner than I, but was unable to communicate that to me. I am so grateful he was there, but what if he hadn't been able or willing to do that? What would we have done with Mom? I'm so glad I didn't have to answer that question, because I really don't know.

My brother kept his place up the road, but stayed with Mom most of the time. His was not a joy-filled task. In Mom's Alzheimer mind, she didn't think she needed any help and she thought her son was her nephew who was down on his luck and she was letting him stay with her to help him out. In reality, his being there bought us time to figure out a longer-term plan, because she couldn't stay alone, and she wouldn't allow anyone else to stay with her.

Mom was kind to my brother most of the time, I think, but sometimes she was downright mean to him. A stroke had taken my brother's ability to speak years earlier, and Mom would yell at him asking him why he wouldn't talk to her. Heartbreaking.

So, we needed to figure out what to do with Mom. Mom and Dad had long-term care insurance so that they could receive care at home. While the insurance turned out to be of very low quality, and may not have helped much in any event, our problem was really not the insurance, but Mom's inability to understand that she could no longer stay alone, and her resultant unwillingness to allow anyone to stay with her. The combination of her lousy insurance and cash could have allowed her to stay at home, if she would have allowed a caregiver to stay with her.

If you are thinking about staying at home and understand that a caregiver is likely to be needed at some point, my advice is to start before you need the help. Hire someone to visit you and clean up around the house and cook some meals. Find someone you like, someone you trust. That way, when you need them, they are already there. My mom was much more accepting of the roles that people played in her life before she lost her memory, than she was of anyone playing a new role. And, really, who couldn't use a little help around the house?

Living four hours away and working full time did not leave me much time to search for options. I searched on the Internet and made phone calls, while my brother did the footwork on the ground.

Without my brother's work, things would not have worked out the way they did for Mom, and certainly not as well. I was not able to find any homes in Mom's area on the Internet, but my brother found at least two. Encourage your loved ones to seek help from each other and from outside, it makes everything so much easier when you're not alone.

I later had a situation with my boyfriend's father when he needed a caregiver. While his situation was different in that he had his full mental faculties, my search methods did not work in that case either. I did my usual Internet searching and phone calls, but the solution was found by word of mouth from someone in the community who knew local caregivers who charged much less than those in the large organizations.

I urge you to look for all options in your community for assistance of all kinds, and research the ones that seem like possible candidates for your situation. I urge you to consider the strengths and weaknesses of each of your loved ones and attempt to ask of each of them only those things for which they are well-suited.

The first home my brother found was amazing on the surface. It was right in Mom's hometown and it was beautiful and clean. We took Mom to this place and had lunch. The food wasn't so great and when talking to people who worked and lived there, they didn't seem too happy. I thought maybe that was the best we could hope for. But, my wonderful brother set his sights higher and found a place that was better than I could have ever dreamed.

All of the assisted living places offer tours and free lunches, so plan some trips!

We went for lunch at this second home, which was also right in town, and right up the street from Mom's church. Who knew? The food was great and the dining area was as comfortable and light as any cozy restaurant. More importantly, the residents were happy and so was the staff. We knew right away this is where Mom should live. They showed us an apartment that I would be happy to have lived in, and Mom liked it too. In the living room was a large picture window with a beautiful flowering tree outside.

Of course, this wasn't the end of the discussion, because Mom didn't want to leave her home, and the place was expensive, but circumstances made it possible for us to move her there a few weeks later.

If I should develop Alzheimer's, as have many women in my family, I plan to find an assisted living place before I am unable to choose. With Alzheimer's disease, and I have learned, with older people in general, familiarity is very important and provides great comfort, so it is a good idea to find a landing spot well before you reach the end of your journey.

To reiterate, if you are still think that you will stay at home until you die, fine. But at least have a Plan B. Back on the prairie in the 1800s, you could stay in your house with your shotgun on your lap and die there. There are many places where this is no longer allowed. So, if you want to stay in your home, you will need to be fully functional right up to the end or plan ahead for help to come to you.

While it is possible that you may stay fully functional until death, it is not probable. The laws in the state we live in, and our own common sense would not allow our mother to stay alone in her house. If we had left her alone, she would have deteriorated quickly and my brother and I would have gone to jail for elder abuse. If you want to stay in your house, you will definitely need to plan ahead, and, frankly, you may not get your wish in any event. So, the best plan may be Plan B, whatever that is for you. Because when your choices run contrary to societal rules, or your loved ones' best judgment, your original choices may be overruled.

So, either make a solid plan for living at home with the care you need provided, or move somewhere where care is available. Sadly, staying home is the most expensive option, although some planning can reduce this amount. That is a main reason why assisted living has become so popular.

I didn't know anything about assisted living facilities when we started our search. There are many kinds, offering all sorts of terms and services, but they have some things in common.

Generally, assisted living facilities are designed for older people who would like to have more services than those available in a traditional home or apartment, such as housekeeping, meals, and transportation, while still preserving independence.

Although these facilities may seem expensive at first glance, it is necessary to factor in everything they offer. In my Mom's case, her one-bedroom apartment included electricity, water, basic cable, three meals a day, housekeeping, laundry, and shuttle service, plus all kinds of entertainment (from movie nights and makeup classes to country music bands and field trips out for Chinese food) and treats (ice cream often, coffee and popcorn always, and wine occasionally).

So it is not a surprise that the rent seems high, but it seems more reasonable when your only additional expenses are a phone and a car, if you want them. The prices at this place were also *a la carte;* so if fewer services were needed, the cost was lower, and if more were needed, the cost was higher.

For my Mom, we paid for extra services. Her apartment door had an alarm on it so that if she left the apartment a caregiver would find her and see what she was up to. They also checked on her every two hours and came to her apartment for each meal, walked her to the dining room, and returned her to her room after each meal.

The caregivers were wonderful people. They would seat her in the restaurant at a table of other women with memory problems, so she fit right in. When she left her apartment, they would usually find her going out for a walk, and they wouldn't just bring her back, they would walk with her. She was not able to walk far, so they would bring her back around to the lobby area and get her a cup of coffee and she was happy there talking to the receptionist and "helping" her.

See, Mom had worked as an office manager in an accounting firm for 35 years and later she and my dad owned an insurance agency. Mom was a hard worker, and even with her Alzheimer's mind she wanted to work. The receptionist would give her a pile of bills, and Mom would sit and go through them happily for a while and would then "finish up" and go back to her apartment.

The assisted living facility gave my Mom some needed activities and companionship that she had been missing out on because of her condition. It was a much better place for her to be than sitting in a remote house alone with an absent mind. She also had a button she could push in the event of an emergency. I think she drove them crazy with the button.

I am so lucky that my brother was able to stay with Mom, because it took some time to find a place to move her, and longer to find a way to get her to accept moving. I suggest that you not rely on luck, because luck swings both ways.

So, whether you would like to stay at home, live with friends or family, join a retirement community, go to assisted living, or relax in a nursing home, planning is required if you want the choice to be yours.

In this next chapter, I will discuss the issues I had with insurance, one of them being long-term care insurance. If you hope to have the funding to take care of your end-of-life housing, or anything else, insurance may be your best funding source. Read on to see some of the potholes that may lurk ahead on your insurance planning road.

INSURANCE POTHOLES

There are many types of insurance we purchase throughout our lives. In our final days, we need to consider how to maintain the payments for the policies, what types of policies we need to have, the ever-present issue of choosing the right beneficiary, and how much coverage is adequate to cover our projected needs.

The first insurance I had to deal with was Dad's life insurance. The trust documents included a company name and policy number. It would have saved a few steps if the information had included the name of their broker and a phone number. I called the 1-800 number and was told that I would receive a return call. Good luck was with me again. The person who called me back, the insurance broker, was an old friend of Dad's he knew from the days when he sold insurance.

This great guy took great care of me, got the policy through and completed and also attended the memorial service and spoke about his memories of Dad's life. It was nice to have a friendly person deal with financial issues. I never knew that it could be so nice to do business with friends.

I have always been the type of person who keeps business and personal matters separate. I thought that mixing personal relationships with business was unwise and messy. It turns out it has a real upside, and is something to consider. I guess the generations before me knew that. Anyway, it is possible that you can make your loved ones' lives easier by having a friendly relationship with your brokers, agents, bankers, *etc.*

Health insurance

My parents both had Medi-gap insurance that was on auto-pay, so I didn't have any difficulties with that. However, you would do well to ensure that you have insurance, if possible, and let your loved ones know where to find the policies and how to contact the agents. They will also need to know how the premiums are paid. If you have no insurance, or are self-insured, your trusted person needs to know that also.

Auto insurance

My parents' auto insurance was also covered with premiums paid automatically, so that process was handled and I didn't have to worry about it.

Homeowner's insurance

The one surprise that came up with homeowner's insurance, is that Mom and Dad's house was a manufactured home, and they are insured differently than brick and mortar homes. I received the bills so I knew who to call, but when I called to have the bills sent to me, they wanted to know if Mom was not going to be living in the house. It turns out that, at least for that type of insurance, covering an empty home is much more expensive than covering an occupied home. This is something to investigate and plan for if it applies in your case.

Long-Term Care Insurance

Perhaps the largest gap in my parents' plan was the long-term care insurance. I am fairly certain that my parents' plan for their long-term care was not to pay $150 per month ($75 each) for about 30 years for absolutely nothing. That is, however, what they did.

I don't know if they didn't know what they bought, or if they just didn't understand the possibilities in their futures. Since Dad was an insurance broker, I think he did know what he was buying, but he may not have carefully considered what their needs might be or the restrictions on how the insurance might be used.

Their long-term care plan covered a caregiver for five hours a day to a maximum of $12 per hour, and only if they stayed at home. I don't think they considered:

1.   How much caregivers charge. Even in the small, out-of-the-way California town where my parents lived, we could find no $12/hour caregiver. There may have been a friend or other private person available, but we didn't know where or how to find one, and the insurance policy required credentialed people.

2.   How little disposable income they might have. The insurance would cover five hours a day at $12 per hour. What if they needed 24-hour care, as my Mom did in the end? Well, that means you cover the other 19 hours in full plus the amount greater than $12 for the first five hours. Since care is most likely to be needed at the far end of life's road, there may be less funding available by then.

3.   The policy only covered care at home, not in an assisted living facility. Be forewarned that personal caregiving is not part of the package in assisted living centers, and if your insurance won't cover a caregiver, you are on your own, so may have to move to a skilled nursing facility to keep costs down.

4.   The claim process. Even if the insurance would have covered Mom, the claim process was odious. I began the process and actually did get her approved for care, before discovering that Mom would not accept anyone in her home. The company sent a person out to test my Mom to see if she met their standards for a person needing care. The woman who came out asked my Mom all sorts of questions to determine her mental abilities. It was not easy to get Mom to participate, but she did. It was interesting that she couldn't answer simple questions, but there were some fairly complex tests that she aced. She was able to recite the alphabet backwards and spell words backward. I found that interesting from someone who could no longer tell you her phone number.

5.   The nature of Alzheimer's. We pretty well knew that Mom would get dementia, since most of her sisters had, and the only sisters who didn't were schizophrenic, which Mom was not. I don't think any of us knew exactly what that would mean, especially since her sisters had all lived on the other end of the country so we didn't experience their decline. But, if Alzheimer's is a possibility for you, think through your plans for care and any insurance carefully. Mom would not allow anyone to stay with her. She was certain that she didn't need anyone, so why would someone stay there with her? The only reason she let my brother stay was because she thought he needed her and that he was a relative so it was her duty. While Dad was alive he sometimes asked the housekeeper to stay with Mom, but Mom would only tolerate her for a short time after the housecleaning was finished. She seemed to understand that the housekeeper shouldn't stay very long after cleaning the house. If you think you may get Alzheimer's at some point, or that your partner may, you would do well to find a companion before you need one. As discussed earlier, it does seem that people with dementia will usually continue to accept a person who they already know before the disease goes too far.

Despite the failure of my parents' policies, I have heard great success stories about long-term care insurance from others. Before you buy long-term care insurance, consider what the possibilities are for you and then read any policy as carefully as you can to be sure exactly what you are buying.

An additional consideration is to insure your trusted person. While I had no wish to be paid for the services I performed as a dutiful child, I did pay for some things out of my own pocket that I believe should have been covered by the trust. One item that comes to mind, because I am paying it still, is an umbrella insurance policy for myself as trustee of the estate, which is to be kept in force for seven years after the close of the trust.

This is the last of the individual issues to discuss before moving on to the next chapter on your estate plan as a whole. My parents had a trust, so I will discuss specifically what I found there, which will hopefully help you do the best job possible with whichever type of estate plan you have chosen.

TRUST POTHOLES

Now that we have discussed many of the issues surrounding your estate plan, let's look at the nuts and bolts of it, including a trust, wills, powers of attorney, *etc.*

Powers of Attorney

Who will speak for you? Even if you have already decided who will hold your power of attorney and/or be executor or trustee, think about it some more. This may be the most important decision in the process. Consider the strengths and weaknesses of the people you may leave behind.

It is important that the person you choose to make decisions on your behalf be the best person for the job and, make no mistake, it is a job. While siblings and others may become jealous when they know that someone else has been appointed as a trustee or executor or has power of attorney, the position that person is in bears great responsibility and weight.

The person must be strong enough to hold to the decisions that you want, even if others want to impose their own will or if outside forces work against them. The person must also be resilient enough to work with your other loved ones and outside people so that your wishes will be honored and so that family and friends can remain family and friends, and your estate can be a process that leaves a stronger bond, not a war that breeds divisive bitterness.

Does this person want the job? I can tell you that neither my mom or dad asked me. I didn't even understand what the job was. You may want to fully discuss the possibilities of the job with your chosen person to find out if they are really up for it.

Consider someone outside of the family, if appropriate. It is often the case that this will be a better choice.

Choose an alternate person. You don't know when the crisis will occur, so your first choice may not be available.

In our case, the power of attorney was traditional. My brother, being the eldest son, had the power of attorney originally, but he had illnesses that disabled him and made it necessary to switch the power to me.

I suggest appointing just one person, and an individual alternate or alternates, one at a time. In our case, I was the sole power of attorney holder during my parents' lives, and was co-trustee with my stepsister for the trust. This worked out okay for us, since my stepsister was willing to let me handle the details for the most part, and I kept her informed of everything that was going on but, even with an amicable situation like ours, it would have been simpler and less time-consuming with just one trustee. I shudder to imagine the misery we would have suffered if we fought through the process.

My stepsister and I live about two hours apart, and each and every task we needed to undertake required both of our signatures, usually notarized. When possible, I would have separate sets of papers sent to each of us and we would return them separately. However, on numerous occasions this was not possible and the papers would be sent to me, and then I would send them to her, and she would sign them in front of a notary and send them back to me, so I could send them where they needed to go.

Another consideration is how free your trustee is to take care of this business. While I have a situation where I am free to go to a notary and get things signed, my stepsister had a more rigid job situation and was in a carpool, so it was very difficult for her to deal with the paperwork and notaries.

Dad's Durable Power of Attorney indicated that he didn't want extraordinary means used to keep him alive if two doctors agreed there wasn't much of a chance for meaningful survival. Well, that is a specific situation that didn't happen to us. We really could have used more clarity about his wishes. Giving as much guidance as you can will not only ensure that you get what you want, but also will relieve the people you leave behind of the burden of making life-and-death decisions. Instead of making heartbreaking decisions, they will simply be sharing your wishes with others. What a blessing to give to those you leave behind!

Mom and Dad made a pretty good plan for us. They had a trust, powers of attorney, durable powers of attorney and wills, and I am forever grateful that they did. I just regret that there were so many things that weren't covered. My parents' trust was originally split between four children, my Mom had two and Dad had two. However, Dad's son died much earlier and so his share was to be given to a charity which was founded and run by Dad's brother.

Non-Money Items

Fulfilling the requirements of the trust would have been much easier if it had been more specific about non-money items. There were four equal beneficiaries, and it is simple and non-controversial to split up money four ways. You just do the math.

Even the house was not too difficult, although I can see how it could have been. We all thought it would be nice to keep it in the family, but none of us could afford to buy out the others and, since one of the beneficiaries was a charity, we would have had to pay cash for that portion. Also, the house was not really suited to any of our needs. In the final accounting, we all decided that despite the sentimental value, it made more sense to sell the house.

In a different situation I can envision the opportunities for all kinds of fighting and spiteful bickering among beneficiaries, and people who think they should be beneficiaries. I suggest in your trust that you direct the house to be sold or make some other specific provision for it. If you put it in writing, the ones left behind don't have to fight about it.

The sale of our parents' house was a piece of cake. In a different market, however, there could be arguing about price, timing, *etc*. Good fortune smiled on us again. The market was heading back up after a crash, and we found a good realtor and put it on the market for the price that Zillow® had placed on it.

We received an offer within days, and the sale was completed the same year my mother passed on. This was a great relief for me, since I was the primary co-trustee, and the trust would have to stay open until after tax time the year following the sale of the house. This saved my stepsister and I from having to be trustees for an entire extra year.

Once the house was sold, it became a money item. The cars, the jewelry, the furniture, dishes, wedding rings, art, *etc.* were more difficult to sort out.

For us, the cars were the most difficult part, I think. Dad's personal items went to his one surviving child, and we all agreed she could have his Suburban, since we didn't want it and she already had the trailer that Mom and Dad pulled with it. Although the trailer was originally listed in the trust, Dad gave it to her before his death, and we were all okay with that.

There was still Mom's car, furniture, and other items from the house. Most of the jewelry and dishes and knickknacks are being held for a time when their granddaughters can take them. We did split up the remainder of the belongings but to this day I feel uncomfortable about the distribution, and somewhat guilty about the things that I received. I recommend that you designate the recipients of all of your belongings, or direct that they be sold, so that your loved ones are freed from those decisions.

Remember, everything doesn't need to be even or "fair." You get to decide. Think out of the box. Be inventive and bold. Perhaps consider giving everything to your most generous beneficiary, so that he or she will then have the opportunity to give out your belongings to the others, making the giver feel great and the receivers feel grateful. There's no answer that fits every situation. Just make it easy on those left behind to be loving to you and to each other. That's what really matters.

I was very fortunate that Uncle Neal, who headed up the charity that was our co-beneficiary, allowed me to do what I needed to do without intervention or argument. I asked if he was okay with the children keeping personal items without paying the charity for the cost of the items, and he said that whatever I decided was fine with him. He told me that he was grateful that I was handling his brother's estate so well and happy that the charity was receiving such abundance from the estate.

While the situation ended well for us, there are so many problems that we could have had, and that your loved ones may face if too many issues are left to be decided later.

Once death occurs, the trust becomes an integral part of the funeral/memorial/burial plan, which will be more specifically covered in the following chapter. For some of us, this part of the plan doesn't matter, so we skim over it, thinking that at that point we will be gone and are not interested in what happens after that. For others, burial and funerals or memorials are extremely important and need to be handled in specific ways.

If you are part of the latter, you are already interested in making plans that will ensure your wishes are respected. If you are in the first group, I urge you to stop skimming and start planning, for the sake of those left behind. Memorials, funerals, and burials all play an integral role in helping people to grieve loss and to move forward after the death of a loved one.

FUNERAL POTHOLES

Right at the start of this chapter, I want to say that you must write down your personal information and share it with your trusted person. When you pass from this earth, your loved ones need to know little things, such as where your parents were born and what your mother's maiden name was. I didn't know these things!

Now, on to the funeral plans. A standard estate plan will usually cover this part pretty well.

People run the gamut from minimal to extraordinarily grandiose in their desires and beliefs about burial or other disposition of their remains. It is important to communicate those desires. If the people handling your funeral choices have different beliefs or values regarding burial, and if what happens at that point is important to you, it is vital that you prepare in advance to make it happen.

Your choices may hold no weight at all if you don't have them in writing, signed and sealed, and held by someone who will honor them. If the details following death are not important to you, I urge you to make some kind of a plan to have a get-together of remembrance to bring your loved ones together and help them to say goodbye.

"Burial" Options

I know there are people who arrange their own burials. If you are going that route, I would urge you to think about the process that may occur when you pass away and the questions that will be put to your loved ones, as well as the decisions and tasks they will be asked to undertake. Look closely. As with some other types of estate plans, these may be designed more toward making a person feel as though they are covered in their time of need so they will pay up, and not so much toward easing the process for those left behind.

My parents' plan was neither formal, nor elaborate. It was simple. My mother had always told me that she wanted to be cremated and she didn't care what we did after that; she would be gone anyway. The trust documents reflected her choices and Dad's.

After Dad passed away, I was asked by the hospital workers who would be picking him up. How the hell should I know? They showed me many choices and I chose the least expensive cremation services, since that was in accordance with the wishes expressed in the trust.

Shortly thereafter, I spoke with Mom and Dad's trust attorney, who was also their friend, and he told me that Dad had contacted him earlier in the year and wanted to change the trust to say that he didn't want to be cremated and he wanted to be buried in the veteran's section of the local cemetery. Well, it was now too late to honor his wishes about the cremation, but my brother went to the cemetery and picked out a very nice plot on a hill in the veteran's section that overlooked trees and grass. Quite lovely, if you like that sort of thing. And, I guess Dad did like that sort of thing, so we purchased the plot, which automatically came with room for Mom.

Next thing I know, I get the call asking what I want done with Dad's ashes. I picked them up and kept them in my car for a couple of weeks because I had no idea what I should do with them until the plot was secured. I couldn't leave the ashes with Mom, because I was not at all sure what she might do with them. I drove the ashes around in my car for three or four weeks until my brother's fiancé agreed to keep them at her home until a decision was made. Having the ashes in my car was a little weird, but oddly comforting too. I felt like Dad was with me.

I have since found out that people often do interesting things with the ashes. I met a woman who took her parents in urns while traveling around the country on vacation. She took pictures of the urns at each tourist spot. I have met people who split the ashes up among several places or several people. Everyone who has shared these stories with me has found comfort in their choices about "burial" methods so, if you are thinking along these lines, you are not alone. When I took Dad's ashes out of my car, I felt kind of lonely for a time.

My wonderful brother had found that great plot where Dad could be laid to rest. It took a bit longer to get a headstone. My time was being spent working to get my mother situated and her matters in order. My brother felt prompted to handle the headstone situation himself when he visited the grave on Veterans Day and found that each grave had an American flag on it, but Dad's did not. Turns out they only put the flags on graves with headstones. So, my brother decided that he didn't want any more official holidays to go by without a headstone.

There are many choices for headstones, but since my brother took the lead, I stayed out of it and my brother and his fiancé chose the stone. I am so glad the two of them took that weight off of me; it was really one thing too many. Suffice it to say here that we purchased a nice headstone and put it on the grave.

Memorial/Funeral

In the midst of all of this, the pastor of Mom and Dad's church was urging me to plan the memorial for Dad. He said the church would do it for free and that I just needed to decide how I wanted it. How would I know?

Keep in mind, I was trying to figure out what to do with a mother who could not take care of herself. I really did not feel at all prepared to deal with a memorial and had no experience with such things. But, I didn't feel as though I had a choice, so I set a date, found my old email list from the party, and invited people to a memorial. Thankfully, Mom and Dad's friends at the church all invited each other so that was covered.

I spent the next week or so gathering photos and putting together a slide show for the memorial. That was really all I had to do. I am so grateful for the people at the church for putting together such a nice spread of food and drink and attending the service and supporting us.

My brother put together a flyer and put it up around their hometown to invite other people they knew in town for whom we had no contact information. Dad was loved in town and there were quite a few people at his service.

The memorial was kind of a blur for me. I didn't think I did such a great job of planning it, but I received praise and flowers and cards. The approval of my dad's family meant the world to me.

Dad's burial was bittersweet, but there were no potholes there. Two workers at the cemetery dug a hole, put the ashes in a weird little container that looked like a dollhouse, glued it shut, and put it in the hole. My brother, Mom, and I stood by watching. Then the workers asked us if we wanted to add some dirt. That was completely unexpected for me, but it felt kind of right. I shoveled, my brother shoveled, and then we asked Mom if she wanted to shovel, and she did. I don't know if she understood completely, but she seemed to feel some peace about it.

Mom's memorial proceeded on the same track as Dad's, and her burial was similar and uneventful.

Burial is the end for all of us, and largely thought of as the last part of your estate plan, but the trust work will continue on long afterward for your trusted person and beneficiaries. Make it all easier for them if you can. Pave carefully the end of your road! The worksheet included after this chapter will help to get you started. Do it now!

IN CLOSING

The key to the process is communication. The successes we had during my parents' end-of-life journey were largely a result of the things that had been communicated in advance, and the failures were largely due to those things that were not. Communicate with those you love for these reasons and because, in the end, it is all that really matters.

Keep in touch. Our family members fought with each other, complained about each other, disapproved of each other, but we also visited each other, threw parties for each other, helped each other, and one of my parents' most loving gifts to all of us was that they made the best plan that they could to make the way as well-paved as possible for those they left behind.

ABOUT THE AUTHOR

K.D. Marley is a third-generation Californian, who has mostly squandered her life, while working, and attempting to entertain everyone she meets with her sarcastic sense of humor. She does like to help people though, and so was tailor-made for trusteeship. As with most things, she didn't plan too much in advance for her parents' end-of-life journey, and learned these lessons in the scalding forge of urgent necessity. The stress of it nearly killed her. She currently splits her time between the northern California coast and the San Joaquin Valley, and works as a patent prosecution paralegal.

Thank you so much for purchasing this guide to the end of your journey. I hope that others will be more wise than I and learn from my experience. As I like to say, you are welcome to my advice, I'm not using it anyway.

Happy Journey!

I would love to hear your feedback and any suggestions you have for how to make the next version of this book even more helpful. Please contact me at kate@kdmarley.com, and visit my website and blog at www.kdmarley.com. Stop by any time!

K.D.

ESTATE PLAN TRANSFORMATION WORKSHEET

I had planned to put together a checklist, but checklists are discrete, defined boxes, and what we need to do here is think out of the box, extrapolate. So, while I have placed some general categories here, please use them only as a guideline for your own brainstorm. Storm away!

<u>Generally</u>
1) What will your loved ones do, specifically, when they get the call that you have suffered a fall and are in a coma? That your memory is so bad now that you can't take care of yourself? That you have died?

2) What can go wrong with your current plan?

3) Are the recommendations you received (if any) suited for your particular situation?

4) How will the people who find you incapacitated know who to call?

5) Did you choose the right person for power of attorney?

6) Did you make your wishes clear enough?

7) Do you want to have a trust?

8) Are you ill?

9) Are there family illnesses which are likely to befall you?

10) Are you keeping information from your loved ones?

11) If not, are your loved ones in denial about it anyway?
12) Write it down.

<u>Medical</u>

1) Which hospital, doctor, alternative practitioner do you prefer? Will these practitioners and organizations provide information to your loved ones and listen to your trusted person? Sign papers if you can.

2) What medications, alternative therapies, and vitamins do you take? Who will speak for you to support your continuing any particular therapy if you cannot speak for yourself? Is that person convinced that you need any of that? They may love you, but not agree with you. Think about that.

3) How is your medical care paid for?

4) What kinds of care do you want/not want to receive if you are ill? Be specific. When the time comes, do you want hospice, or do you want everything humanly possible to be done for you?

5) Who do you want by your side while you are ill? Who don't you want there? Are there people you want at your memorial but not with you while you are ill? Vice versa?

Contacts

1) Gather contact information for family, friends, clergy. Who can help with what?

2) On-line passwords and user names?

3) Who does your hair, your nails, cleans your house? Which restaurants do you frequent? Who do you like there?

<u>Banks</u>

1) Where do you do your banking? Where is your money? Do you have any money? Do you receive government benefits? Are any available to you? Bring your trusted person to the financial institutions and have them added to your account in ways that will allow them to do what needs to be done without taking on liability for your financial situation.

Government

1) Department of Motor Vehicles. Get a login.

2) Social Security. Are you married? How will you make ends meet if you lose your spouse, or vice versa?

3) Do you receive benefits? From which government entity? Be specific.

Housing

1) Where do you want to live? Now? Later? Does this place have what you need? What if your mobility becomes limited? Are there transportation services available? Other services? Check out options in your community. Or outside your community. Check out some places and write down your thoughts.

Insurance

1) What kinds of insurance do you have? How are the premiums paid? Do you have enough? Do you have too much? Find out. Meet with a broker and bring your trusted person.

Health insurance

Auto insurance

Homeowner's/Renter's insurance

Long-Term Care Insurance

Other Insurance

<u>Trust</u>

1) Who do you trust? Will that person fight for your wishes? Is that person strong enough and resilient enough to be your trustee or executor? Should you hire someone instead? Who?

<u>Non-Money Items</u>
1) Do you have a special piece of jewelry that you would like to give to a specific person, or knick knacks or other items? I urge you to not be so concerned about everything being equal for your beneficiaries. If one of them finds something you have special to them, give it to them. Try to find out what might be special to each person. The money can be split equally, but other things are difficult and if it is your decision, everything is easier on those left behind.

Funeral/Memorial

1) "Burial" Options. Cremation? Embalming? Viewing? Spreading? What do you want?

2) Who do you want to handle your funeral/memorial? Any particular people for particular tasks?

3) Funeral or memorial or both? Where? Who will preside? Who will attend?

4) What do you want to wear?

www.ingramcontent.com/pod-product-compliance
Lightning Source LLC
Chambersburg PA
CBHW070257190526
45169CB00001B/451